Where It Will
Copyright © 2024 Anthony Botti

Cover Art by Andrew Hilliard
Original art information can be found at http://tinyurl.com/msafrnmr

The fonts used are Garamond and Grandview
The cover font is Elza

Gnashing Teeth Publishing
242 East Main Street
Norman AR 71960

Printed in the United States of America

ISBN 979-8-9875694-5-0

Non-Fiction: Poetry

Gnashing Teeth Publishing First Edition

Advance Praise for *Where It Will*

Anthony Botti's poems look unflinchingly at mortality and the seasons of life, finely tuned to the rhythms of the natural world; internally and externally, Botti hears truths spoken to him, through him: "Your voice unspools inside me knitting /on the porch while bats crisscross/ the yard. The blow-up// that morning at Dad's funeral is as burnished/ as a scar on that old elm tree." He writes of death (of his parents, the deaths of friends, death of love and expectation) as lyrically as he does of the wider world he senses around him, finding strength and security in an undeclared partnership: "Behind the frozen pane/ the day glistens on the windowsill, tracks of deer in the creased/ snow. How close they came while I was sleeping." The meditative poems in *Where It Will* hold stories of love—romantic love, familial love, love for the earth and its creatures—as well as of heartbreak, standing at the crossroads of holding onto or letting go of love.

Valerie Duff, author of *Aquamarine* (Lily Poetry)

Anthony Botti's *Where It Will* flashes with brilliant, intimate portrait sketches of those loved and lost due to disease. We are privy to the yearning and regrets of a lifetime ensconced in poetry that portrays details with novelistic accuracy. Botti takes us to the marshes of the Netherlands where horses romp and through the dark nights of the soul, "All night I live with cracking branches" (from "December Night") and "words that fell over us like confetti" (from "While You Were Away"). Longing is expressed through regret and memories "one notation at a time"(from "Reading My Father") and we want to find out more through these poems which are very much like secret notes and letters to the past.

Susan Kay Anderson, author of *Mezzanine*
(Finishing Line Press)

Where It Will is a collection that honors how we love each other, if we are so lucky as to love, exploring the difficulties in accepting our own failings and of those who we share our lives with. These poems are offerings—"small fragments," Botti writes in "Last Will and Testament"—to parents, lovers, friends lost to AIDS. Botti draws sharp lines around the mundanity of daily routines, the ebb and flow of long-term relationships, and the inevitability of loss. In terse confessions, regret and desire pull at each other as naturally as the moon and the waves, or like a ship at sea—no clearer than in my favorite poem in the collection, "Ahab's Crew": "Never again/ would we drop into our bodies/ with the same aching."

Chris Ankney, author of *Hearsay*

Where It Will

per mio padre
inciso in ogni memoria

for Jon, always there

Table of Contents

Like a white stone in a deep well
one memory lies inside me.
I cannot and will not fight against it:
it is joy and it is pain.

Section 1

August Heat

What I want is never simple.
It's August, the garden is moaning.
I know I am at fault pruning these roses in second
bloom that knows what is coming, a short
lifespan like happiness.

When we first met in Cambridge, I expected you to dig up
the loneliness carried deep inside me.

On my knees in this border bed, I hold out a clump
of dirt like a few useless words of apology to persuade
you to come back out in the moist air, to roll over
for you like the farmer's cat on its back
in the high bushes. When will I stop

asking you to diagram a way out of my sadness?
Yes, we traveled all of Italy for two months, you taught
me to make the perfect dry martini, how to split a cord of wood.

Again, this afternoon, I failed
at sight reading your affection in the yard,
your signals of solace. The glare in the August sun sends a false
impression, the rose's deep red color a perfect
disguise until I turn around to see the petals falling to earth.

I ask too much
like how I dare these blossoms not to wilt
in the afternoon heat, their hooded
gaze never looking away from what approaches.

On The Tide Line

On the vanishing beach at the tip
of the Cape, you stretch out naked
smooth in the sand, shameless
as a snake in your tanned skin.
Terns swoop down overhead
to shoo us away, their brave nests
on the tide line.

An hour passes staring at the sea, changing
color in the waves. We plunge
in the Atlantic, the cold
grabs at our bodies. My legs lock
around your waist. Something stops
me, pushes away your hunting hands inching
down my curved spine. I yank up
the swim trunks slipping down
my hips from fear stored
in my body and pull back, tangled
in the brown kelp
of red tide.

Back on shore, I look toward the sun,
already going down, dry off
in the fast heat.

Man To Man

The alarm clock goes off at 5:30 a.m. You push back
clean sheets. No more rolling on the bed
in early morning. After coffee you button
a white oxford shirt, rub both hands down
your gray flannel trousers. What still excites you?
Go ahead: say what you're thinking.
Before leaving for work,
you stand by the door, your frightened
lips facing me. My tense fingers murmur down
your shoulder as you move forward,
past me after so many years in the same
house. I follow you, but not by your side.
I know I cannot force my loneliness
that I call love onto you. The screen door bangs,
you walk away across the yard. Outside
the snow is crusted hard. We know we cannot
give each other any more or any less.

The Red Line, Boston

They have left offices in the jagged
darkness, carved out privacy on this subway car,
rubbing shoulders in their seats. Some read,
others look on. A goose-necked woman in a suede hat
holds *The Great Gatsby* close to her face. The walls
of the train are veiled in cosmetic ads.
Two businessmen flip through crackling
pages of the *Boston Globe*, cloaked
behind the front cover that reads
in large bold print *OSAMA BIN LADEN IS DEAD.*
At the Central Square stop
a can of beer wrapped in a brown paper bag
rolls off the seat. The baby clutching his stuffed
rabbit sleeps on his mother's sagging
shoulder as she stares into the world
of her reveries. She'll wake him when they cross
Longfellow Bridge. By the emergency exit
a girl with waist length hair in a tight braid,
polished shoes, knits one, purls one, stitching
a gray scarf. The train runs from one dark
tunnel into another. Commuters propped up
on their seats counterfeit the long hours at work,
carried to the end of the line.

Then

I do not know what led to this, or when it began.
Of course, I have changed since we first unpacked
our book bags on Divinity Avenue, cracking

those history texts open to ancient Rome
in Widener Library. Twenty years later you sit
on a wicker chair across the porch, arms crossing your chest.

The dog watches us from his bed. Two hawks skirmish
in midflight, dropping to the meadow
nearby. When we look away through the tangle

of trees, I look to the past, to those days living
on Hampshire Street. I would like to speak
to you of that memory. Your sun bleached

bangs tumbled over your smooth forehead, sun
swelling across your bare shoulders, there
on the wrinkled bed, absorbing the weight

of your leg on mine. These things tucked
away would not have lasted long anyway, years
of experience taught me that as we fell

into this rhythm of silence. All summer
the house has baked. Now we say so little,
shutting the hard talk out.

Copenhagen

You don't apologize for being hard
to know. A loneliness breaks out
between two people after years together
that can't quite be put down.

While I paced the back porch
last night listening for the rain to stop,
you walked narrow streets

in another country in sunlight. By morning
only lowing cattle broke

the monotony of rain. *I don't mind
being away from you. That's not
the problem.* We speak
to each other in the silence which separates
us. *Have it your own way.*
Summer has already come and gone. Still

you and I do not span
the distance inside the passing days.

Now you've come back
in September, still hoarding
your silence. I toast *skal* as you taught
me in your native tongue,
though your shot of Aquavit
remains untouched on the table.

Us

The day after Thanksgiving you're bent
over the arts section of the *Globe*, a choke
comes into your voice, *I don't feel so young
anymore*. Only yesterday sprawled out on the carpet,
we mapped out our Christmas holiday on a big atlas, still
acting like teenagers planning a field trip. I suspect

it has something to do when you went back
to the old neighborhood last month, your pink stucco
house in the Sunset District. Any man would feel out
of sorts with the vanished boy playing
in the next room where you'd grown up in.
Remember that first year together you would

chuckle when I chatted about my adolescent years, tracing
my life out of a Henry James novel in the coal
fields of landlocked PA, or conjugating irregular French
verbs aloud on Nana's back steps. The only time I got
to be a kid has been with you these last ten years. So
when you coughed out your youth was over, two children

receded into the thick woods, hand in hand
stunned by the rough voice of a witch calling out to us.

January Blizzard

On the first blizzard of the season, you get up
to poke the embers to keep

the fire from going out. You pick
over my fumbling words. I twist

your long sentences of explanation. We wait
for the other to give up, this tango of abrupt

turns binds us together tonight.
You crouch to put another log on the fire.

Firelight throws shadows of our stubborn
backs on the white wall behind us.

Afterwards

For a long time, you fidgeted
with your ring. Why
couldn't I just say *fight it out
with me*. Afterwards
we separated.
You went up to the loft
to escape in a book. I fussed
downstairs, stirred
soup in the kitchen, carrying on
last night's quarrel in silence.
That night we stayed
out of each other's way,
alert to every creak
on the floorboards in the cabin.
At sunrise I looked out
the bedroom window into the gnarled
apple trees, their shadows on the crusted
snow. My fingernail scratched
at the star frost built up
on the corner of the glass pane.

Lesson In Birdwatching

I flip through holiday cards by the bay window, that ritual cord
every December bonding my dispersed

family. His face springs out at me from an old
photograph that my sister has enclosed.

On the back of the black and white,
my father's handwriting curls at the bottom

right corner *Summer 1976 on the front porch.*
Last August his sudden death was like falling down

a flight of stairs. In the last few months I've sat guard
over my father's old letters sealed up

in a drawer, the knotted ball of his waiting
words to me. This afternoon in a wedge

of sun counting chickadees and blue jays
at the feeder during the annual Christmas bird count,

I ask what he would now say to me
here at my cold desk.

Has anyone ever seen an aging bird?
I stare out at the winter sun

dropping to the west, only to be startled by a thump
of soft breast against the glass pane.

The bird smacks the ground, unmoving. Bolting
outside, I cradle the body with its wild

heart still racing in my fingers. Will I dig
a grave in the icy ground? Or just cover it

with snow? All at once, it lifts off
so close I feel its wing brush my cheek

to a high branch on a pine, its figure just a blotch
of red against the green. My eyes follow this cardinal

crossing open sky. I stretch out
my right arm, as if I too had wings to let go.

Mirror

This morning I see you in my raised
brow and forehead lines caught
in the bathroom mirror.
How I'm startled at the sad cast
to your brown eyes. I know you, father,
better now that you have been dead
these last two years. I think
of you at the age I am now, crossing
the campus on cold autumn mornings.
You have returned in my tired
face as the open-jawed razor cuts
the morning shadow, stroke
by stroke seeing you in midlife for the first
time. Looking at you
looking.

The Rift

after Jon's return from Antwerp

You have come to the landscape of winter passing
by what is left by the ravens, a dead squirrel's coat
thick for the December chill. From the old dirt road, I look

for you in the early morning when you are out alone
on the farm. By the red barn a Belgian workhorse, head bowed,
travels the fence line to you, its mouth opening
at the sight of a hand, your outstretched
palm ready to feed it carrots. This lame

horse stands there like a blessing, not questioning
your silence, however long. The mare's nostrils

open, her soft nose rubs up your arm nuzzling away
your fear, this brief time when nothing is asked
of you in the deserted field. In the unhurried sun, you come
to learn you burn like stars, even
in full daylight. I see on your face

what I too am thinking, what you are remembering of the rift
inside our silence. *What you give me must be enough*,
I tell myself. Untangling the horse's matted mane,
you're back with a cold knowledge that everything is just
as we left it. By the broken-down tractor, you stood
a long time in the freezing wind.

Dog Commands In Spring

Tangled at my feet,
Ernie whines to smell the earth thawed
after a long winter, taking me for a walk
in the Boston Public Garden. Off leash

by the pond, he tears a wide orbit
around me once, twice,
three times before collapsing in a satisfied

sigh on new grass. What's it like not
to mull over every worry, just
bound forward? Jumping up,

he gives himself a violent
shake I wish I could do when things pile up
on me--this too, this too. He rushes ahead, straining
the leash, chases down
the high music of a fresh smell. Words have no weight
set side by side with his pug mind.

Dragging me home an hour later, he wears
his impatience with me in fast
snorts, looks up for the usual treat, his teeth
careful of my fingers. Back

inside, he leans against the red
pillow bracing himself as if against a strong
wind in a near standstill with a cold
stare at me. He opens and closes his mouth, the way
he does when I imagine he considers some great

mystery. His stub nose pokes up
in the air sniffing out
the truth about me while I compile my lists, the kind
sure to keep me up until midnight.
I get up and down off the couch. Ernie plops
on my lap instructing me: sit, stay.

Overwinter

Ash Wednesday

I expect disaster when opening up
the cabin after a long period away, burst
pipes, dead mice, fallen trees. Seldom

am I ready after the raw silence
under the high snow on the first
balmy day in the Berkshires.
With no winter to hide in, I shed my thick
coat like skin. In the yard

given over to a sudden thaw, the dog noses around
green sprouts that emerge from the clotted
mud, never imagined anything to have survived
in the garden this spring. How do I attempt to live out
the Lenten season? I'm learning to clear

myself as I clear out these beds, a new muscle
stretches in the rising temperature. A shrivel
of red leaf squeezes its way up
through loam, stem by stem
unfolding the whole mystery. As April

heals drinking in the sun, shy fern
fronds smash through cold nights, craving what
the earth makes poised
to shoot up in its own time, to speak.

That First Summer

After the tide swept
away the broken shells, we soaked
in the constant sun on our backs,
living like nomads day to day,
each day through. That
first summer we wanted nothing
more from each other, just
this. The picture we drew in the sand,
signed our names to, washed
away by noon. You inched
closer to me on the plaid quilt, traded our salt
lips. Afterwards you fell asleep
open-mouthed. By the time the sun slung
low, your long legs danced
in the surf. I stood waist-deep
in the ocean, the waves drowning out
my words to you, an hour before we had to board
the last train home to Boston. That was more
than twenty years ago at Manchester-by-the-Sea.
I had not yet done things that would need forgiving.

from a summer journal
Blackhead Trail, Monhegan Island

On the third day we woke
to drenching fog
and the rising arguments
of waves in Elfin Cottage.

By noon, the sun lifts
the cover over the Atlantic

sky. It's time to set out to hike around
the island. Up on the cliff's edge, we stumble
on a young gull out of its nest, licked
by the salt air, wobbling
on a thin ledge.

In the blowing mist
the sea washes up the brusque
dialogue from this morning, the wind
taking what's unsaid

between us. On the trail the afternoon opens up.
Splintering through the tips
of the pines, the light is there waiting
for us. Too hot to talk, I hold out
my hand. My look back and a nod of your chin
seem the best form of conversation
where the surf below comes in loud.

We turn left to start down
to the shoreline. What is swept
away, erased on the coast
is as important as what remains. Wave

upon wave washes up kelp,
a crab leg, a stone, perfectly round in our private
silence. I put this one in my pocket. By high tide
the sand is swabbed clean.

Section 2

There is nothing to do now but wait
notebook, December 1982

I scribbled this sentence down the margin when I lived
in the back room of my father's house on the hill, coming out

for the dinner ritual in the cold kitchen where we faced
one another but saw nothing as though we sat

on public benches in a park. Afterwards
mother withdrew with a migraine, in pain

resting on the last few stairs. For two days she cordoned
herself off in the spare bedroom, her face floating

at the window. During the blizzard of '82, I tucked
myself away in the root cellar stuffing winter bulbs

in a metal box, the silence in the damp dark
breathing, *how they try to grow without light,*

white sprouts putting out life. Biding my time on the dirt
floor, I played out ways to spar with him, words that pricked

my tender throat. After New Year's, I would leave
throbbing to feel my days grow weightless.

Photograph In Changing Light

A bleached-out photograph preserved
by accident between the pages of a book
jogs my memory this morning, fastening
me to my youth. I was not

looking at the camera when someone snapped
that picture. I stared off to the side gazing
at aunts who sipped coffee, made jibes
about not showing up

for the holiday meal. I tell myself
old photographs are supposed to be silent.
Why then am I stirred up by how I trembled
that Easter, wounds I never speak aloud?

That winter there were bullies, a new one
and a few from the year before, tormenting
me for the entire school year--- *I'm gonna kill
you, queer.* After classes I hid

in Agatha Christie mysteries in dark
stacks of the school library. I took
their shoves, their punches. I drew
bullies to me, not because I wouldn't fight,

but because they knew I wouldn't report
them. Photographs are so-called
anchors of the objective past, but are unstable
as everything else. Tilting this Polaroid

under the lamp shade, I reassemble the parts
of my eleven-year-old self. By middle school
I had learned pain hurts less when you expect
it at the lunchroom hour.

Ahab's Crew
boarding school, 1980

October flares in western PA.
In rumpled uniforms boys mock
each other around the oak
table, two chairs lean
daringly on back legs.
The schoolmaster shows up

late on black mornings, beret tipped
wide on his high forehead, tweed
jacket dangling from his hunched
shoulders. Twice he clears his throat,
a voice more trusted
than their own fathers, before reading out
loud from *Moby Dick*. Thin smoke
rises from the hot ember at his fingertips.
Half-listening, they slouch
with their hair curling
round their heads, look up at his moving lips,
pausing to hear how the sailors' long
arms swim elbow deep
through Pequod's barrel
of spermacelli, oily fingers hunt
for their shipmates' hands to hold on deck
in the light of day. By evening,

the housemaster, barefoot
in the common room, calls *lights out*.
Sleepless on slim beds, hungry hands
in the dark hit on eager skin
under crisp white sheets. Never again
would they drop into their bodies
with the same aching.

Hansel Revisited

Stepmother hurried
us off into the black forest, a loaf of dark
rye bread wrapped in a red
handkerchief under Gretel's apron.
After two years of war and food
rationing, I had a hunch

peeking back, the treetops blocked
the sun's rays in the thick
woods. Children just know

when to go along.

The night before stepmother packed us up,
her whiskey breath held back
a bowl of potato soup
after she spied on me with Kurt in the barn. Still,
I stayed up late

in bed hoarding memorized phrases, syllable
by syllable, in French. I would not
have heard Nazi slogans in her midnight
whispers had my stomach
not been so empty. In the dense woods I can still

taste the hard bread I chewed instead
of dropping crumbs on the trail after 40 paces.

Candy-starved, I marched up to the cottage.
Who is nibbling at my gingerbread
shutters? Her cozy voice hypnotized

me, lured me into the closet
with apple cake, cinnamon overpowered
the foul odor sinking in the air. By the time Gretel

killed the witch in the oven's hungry mouth,
I had come to learn a witch
could turn up anywhere.

On back roads we came upon brown shirts gobbling
red apples. By dark

we had reached
a crossing that I recalled
before the war. All night
we hid in the tall grass, Allied planes
overhead. At daybreak

I meant to set off alone
for the French village across the German border.
In the sudden

morning Gretel begged me to go back.
What did you expect, Gretel?
We had lain long enough, no longer children
running away in a game of hide-and-seek.
After all that took place, how could you have asked
me to roll over another night in my narrow bed, just

to make a U-turn?
Through the mountain pass I found myself disoriented,
no directions, no maps. If I intended
to survive, I could not go back there as I was.

First Bike

Out on the back porch
my father has fallen asleep
before noon, his prayer book
dangling open over the worn
arm of the rocking
chair. The rattle
of his half breath exhales
after years without many wishes
granted to him. In a pool of light,
my gaze is pinned
on his younger profile
against the PA sky, staring out
at childhood. I look past
the waves of clouds and flash back
to skinny legs pumping
my new purple bicycle, this time
without training wheels,
as I wobble down
the gray sidewalk
to the winding road
ahead, leaning
against his right hip.
On the front stoop
my sister pouts
over my shiny banana handle
bars. If I peddle fast enough,
his sadness will not catch up
to me, his firm hand
still holding
the rim of the bike seat.

He hangs on like a heavy
shadow, his cigar breath
on my tanned skin. Laughing,
I try to pull ahead, tucked
under my tongue I shout,
let go, let go.

On The Front Porch

I lived on a dead end
street at 1888 Brett Lane. Supper
done with, mother washed
and dried the dishes, an old dishrag
hanging over her left shoulder
as she slouched into the rocker, her cigarette
flaring like a steady gaze. The German
shepherd snuffled in the wet
leaves under the elm
tree. A sprinkler whirled
on the neighbor's lawn.
And my sister twirled her baton
on the front steps. I could tell
father wanted to be left
alone on the chaise lounge asserting
a cold control over us, his bourbon balanced
on the banister. I rolled
an earth marble in the palm
of my hand. Cicadas droned
in the pines, and Nixon's impeachment
played in the background
on the kitchen TV. Scraps of hard
feelings between my mother and father covered
the porch floor. Even our house looked
sad in the way their bodies were sad
that summer. The nights had already grown
cool. The sun refused to set.
At thirteen I would stare at the long wall of gold
light on the peeling clapboards,
listen for the coal train
slipping through the Allegheny mountains.

Family Dinner, 1972

My father's clenched fist
slams down hard, silence falling
at the dinner table.
The tablecloth jerks up
skipping plates. My water glass tips
over, rolling off, and Mom's jaw
thrusts out, getting up to mop
the checkered linoleum
floor. His nervous fingers rake back
thick bangs from his eyes blazing
down at Philip's muddy
soccer cleats, my brother's bowed
face chewed up in hurt.
I stare down
at my lap laying
down my fork, my legs intertwine
under the chair to lock
up my body.
The refrigerator whirrs behind
me. Earlier my big sister gossiped
about the neighbor's daughter,
laughing wide mouthfuls
of chewed peas. I reach over
to hold her hand
under the chair. Mashed
potatoes steam
on the table. Slip
me through the front
door keyhole or make me
swallow hard not to cry
looking down at the liver
on my dish flapping
at me like an ugly tongue.

The Hush

What I never told you
about growing up near coal fields

that painted the landscape black at the edge
of my town was how my father shouted

lugging his burden of obligations to us all through
the house. Yet when silence did come

to live among the angers of my family,
it was full of the unspoken.

I learned early to arrange a book
before my face, a shield from his husky voice.

Now looking back on those years,
I see my father with a chemistry textbook

at his hip on the way to his classroom lab
carrying his sadness in those sloping

shoulders like an invisible knapsack,
a barricade he built around himself to keep

us from his mute disappointments.
A year later I sit in this yellow chair, look out

at morning's light falling on the brick
sidewalks of Charles Street where the quiet

sounds leave me to stare hard
into the choked silence of his absence.

Visitation

for a boyhood friend

I grew up believing in invisible things like the holy spirit,
the intercession of saints, apparitions of Mary. At 55
why can I only see what's close at hand? Like these bulbs
I planted in clusters last autumn in all the wrong
spots. My fingers crusted with soil poke
at sprouts, weed around them. I imagine what
grows in such darkness, and like a shot
out of the earth, your voice is sent up
through the cracks in the dry dirt. Or is it just
a voice of you in me? *Tony, we were only meant*

to carry each other through our lonely childhood.
You've come looking for me after all this time. Five years ago

as the news came in over the phone that you had lung
cancer, I was in the kitchen preparing a new French
recipe. After these irises were replanted
this afternoon in the hot
sun that pinched my face, I reply:
Yes, I do remember the way we hid
together behind books in the library and sat
by the pond's edge uncovering
we were gay. I've changed
in 30 years. Even back then

I knew I would get rid
of anything that bore the imprint
of that coal mining town, would go far beyond
there. Yet here tending my garden that's never that
far from death, I keep finding the past

with you. Why all those years did we circle around
each other in European capitals never meeting up?
Right now, in the flare of twilight,

I listen one last moment to the yard, the hot
smell of peat locked around me, and a surge
of missing you lodged in my throat. I want to stumble
upon you at that pond once more, and not change a thing.

The Test
Boston Medical HIV/AIDS Clinic, 1991

On Wednesday, it's inconclusive.
You need to repeat the test,
the nurse advises me over the phone.

In a headache of confusion,
I question her *what*
does inconclusive mean?

Rushing me off, *there is an opening*
in the doctor's schedule this afternoon.
He will explain it to you when you come in.

For the next three hours I walk back
streets of Beacon Hill, smoothing a coarse stone
in my front pocket, something to hold on to
in the heat that does not break
as shadows lengthen
on brownstones. Today started

as a collection of trivial details, little
intimacies, a few laughs, never
knowing I was happy, just
another ordinary day that cracked
down the middle. A week

later after repeating the test, I stride out
of the clinic, the doors gliding shut behind me,
sun and pale blue sky.

The friends I outlived, thirty years
later their names tumble
into a numb well.

Cherry Blossoms In Cambridge
portrait of a friend with AIDS, 1992

The last memory I have of you is standing
on Putnam Avenue under trees in late
April, a cluster of flaring blossoms shouted out
to your lover stepping away *come back,*
come back. You bent a branch down
to your face. Leaning up
against the rough bark in the wrinkled
light, I heard you mutter under your breath
go anywhere I cannot
follow you. Later that day a spring storm
brought down a dark afternoon, soft buds smacked
to the ground under a sky torn
by clouds. On Thursday you called
to tell me how the next
day in the shy sun you scooped up
the pink casualties off the brick
sidewalk, rubbing their tight
fists in your palm. Once your diagnosis was let
out, you knew nothing could be brought back
after the blowing rain ripped
through the tree before the modest
shoots had even time to break open.

February Day, Boston
for Ralph

Half past seven. I wake from a dream that brought
back everything, get up in silence to sun
on the calla lily in the vase, a single beam assaulting
the swirled cup. All last night I slept
in fits and starts, curled up
like a leaf into myself after learning
you were gone, how the shared fact
of our childhood was now buried. Yesterday

pent up in this apartment, snow skimmed past
the windows on horizontal waves veiling
the loss, drifts piled up
on the front steps under the high wind. Even
the February air scraped
under the peeling windowsill.
How did our knot

in adolescence slip,
as we separated
after college, writing letters at first,
then phone calls at Christmas, and in the last
few years just Facebook posts? Fixed
in place on that prep school campus, we left
our young lives undisturbed. There
we found in the great books what held
the key to be somebody else, to push forward
at all costs, counting the paces we put
between ourselves and the hometown
where we never fit in. Watching

the last light
leave the windows, I see more clearly, resist
nostalgia. Instead
imagine our mature years apart,
trying out adulthood in different cities. Alone
on this late afternoon, the narcissus bulbs
planted last month in clay pots
split open.

The Recipe

The last time I saw my mother stand at the kitchen
window in our childhood home, she was lining up
ingredients on the Formica countertop. *Teach me*

to make your Italian meatloaf. *There's no recipe,*
she shrugged puffing long
on her cigarette. Two pounds of ground
beef and pork, two eggs. I tried to assess what
quantity of breadcrumbs to write down
before you added chopped parsley, salt

and pepper to that dented stainless steel
bowl. With elbows on the table, I was starting to let
my secrets out about gay life in a new city like doves held
captive too long. *Make sure you drizzle tomato sauce over*
the meatloaf before serving. She held out a wooden spoon
to taste the sauce simmering on a back
burner. A year before we all had just
begun to read about thrush and purplish spots
on legs and faces in NY, the gay bars pulsed
with whispers. I wasn't afraid until I said aloud
they call it a gay cancer dipping hard
bread into the pot of red sauce. She chopped

onion, red pepper, and garlic in perfect
portions. By the sink the radio station played
Michael Jackson's *Man in the Mirror*. She wiped

the cutting board surface clean
before grating the cheese. *The secret*
is to make the loaf not
too dense so pour in a couple of spoonfuls
of sauce at the end. Just dig your fingers deep
in the jumbled-up mixture, all the flavors blended
like my hang ups on that day melding the savory and sweet.
Tapping out another Marlboro from her embossed
case, she answered questions I did not
know I was asking.

Sunday Phone Call

All last night I held conversations with you. You stubbed out
your cigar, striding barefoot into my dream and went on sparring

with me, though your last month in the hospital was silent.
How do I make this a normal Sunday evening?
Make a plate of spaghetti, walk up the dirt
road with the dog, rent a foreign film. Instead, I down
Jameson neat by the woodstove. When the phone rings

in the kitchen, I forget that it can't be you. Remember
Christmas Eve of '68 when you drilled me to repeat
our new telephone number over and over
in the passenger seat, just in case I got lost
among the holiday crowds at Gimbel's Department Store.

Asleep, I hear your voice young again, rallying
fast tennis balls at me across the hot clay court.
Outside geese over the house call in distress, the unbroken
dark pressing around me. It feels like snow. The call tonight
is my sister letting me know that your tombstone
cannot be placed until the earth settles.

The Sick Bed

My father lies face up just beneath
the surface of water reminding me when he used to float
on his back in the pool where he learned to swim
at fifty. He shows no expression now except the wide
eyes saying hard things in his scrambled
mind. Voices rise and fall in the kitchen, his daughters flowing
in and out of the room like the August tide
on the Jersey shore where he chased
us over the hot sand. Two grandsons click
bocce balls in the mowed grass. In the furious heat
his wife and children take shifts at his bedside
each hour to moisten his cracked lips and thick
tongue with pink sponges on paper sticks dipped
into ice water. I pull the shade low, not to allow the glare
of the setting sun to fall on his body. His heavy breath
vibrates in the darkening room. Outside the wind comes up
through the chestnut trees he planted in the backyard.
In the moonless night, fireflies blink at his window,
swallowed in the unmoving dark.

Mission Hill, AIDS Hospice
counseling a client, 1997

Yes, I used to pray, the way mother prayed
at St. Matthew's in Des Moines, head down,
kneeling on hard pews. Back then the mass would
draw me out of dark moods. Today I lie curled
up on a double bed stunned
like a fox in a pen. From the window
I see a piece of the city skyline, breaks
of shadows. This morning my fever spiked,
last night it was vertigo, then nausea
and a nosebleed dripping across the carpet.
It is the third day laboring to breathe between
coughs. The night nurse allowed
my dog Puck to come with me. He cocks
his head turning to the door, his ears stiffen
at the edge of the bed. What
does he hear in the air that I don't?
After some low growls, he goes back
to licking my feet. An uneasy stillness comes just
like the flat gray sky before the hard
rains moved across the Iowa cornfields in late
summer. No one would guess
that I've come back to reading
scripture, not those verses my aunt recited
aloud to betray me to my father, my bruised
hand stretching for the Bible cracked
open to *Psalm 90* on the down quilt.

Last Rites
James 5:14

You came back in a dream, yet
some things still resist remembering even
after 25 years. Yes, we were no longer boys holding
the chalice, ringing bells at the altar. Not
since AIDS when there were no
miracles, no cures. All these years I have circled
around that winter day like a hawk
over a field, never plunging
into the memory. It was late

January 1992. I stood leaning over the bedrail,
a copy of the Bible by your bedside, earmarked
to the epistle of *James*. I questioned
if I should say something about the passage,
steer the conversation in a certain
direction. I knew the chance would not
come again. *Say what you're thinking*, I stopped
myself from blurting out.
That night you fell silent, just too young to outrun
those early shadows. Only tubes and wires hooked up
to monitors ticked, chattered
in ICU. I've never forgotten
our last day, still can

picture holding your hand, swollen
from the IV, morphine dripping
into your arm by the bagful.
All the drugs had failed. I arranged

for a priest to give last rites after your mother insisted
over the phone. By midnight you had already ebbed

away into your private
dreams. Were they full of earlier untroubled
times, perhaps even better an old
romance? Alone with you in those last
hours, your blue eyes went blank,
then dark without last words.

At Prayer
for Mother

Winters are long here, the windows darkened
at this early hour before lighting wood
stoves in the cabin. The phone call

from the hospital where you had undergone
some tests yesterday took
me by surprise, not expecting
to hear your diagnosis. A month

after the first hard frost, crows
circle a corner of sky, the color
of chimney smoke. Charcoal fog
in the thick air spills
across new snow on the freezing
lawn. I will be as resigned

as these bare trees, to wait out
in this unforgiving month, what

comes next by your hospital bed,
as you sleep into winter. The growing
darkness of January widens.

After The Coma

She woke 3 months later with a surgically placed
hole in her trachea. I pull up a chair closer to the bedrail,
her body cramped inside the hospital bed, mangled in plastic
tubing. Two months earlier my older sister fastened
St. Jude and St. Anthony medals, hung on a safety pin
to her loose hospital gown. I examine her blotted

figure up and down,
the same mother who wiggled
herself into a girdle every morning. Unblinking,

she mouths puffs of air to me. I bend down
straining to hear her words over monitors that bleep
and ping. *I'm sorry Mom,*

one more time. Lip reading
would be easier if she had her dentures in,
but they no longer fit. Will I hear again
her malapropisms at the dinner table or that
Marlboro voice that hollered
ye gads when she stabbed her eyes at us?

I pass her a piece of paper, a pen.
Yet her hands are too weak, scratching only faint
lines. Once more she opens her mouth wide

as if screaming, the air bypassing her cords, rendering
her voiceless. That whole day I'm lulled by the rhythm
of fluids dripping through IV tubes. *You must get better,*
there's still so much we need to talk about.

Housekeeping

I never saw my mother in a bathing suit
like other wives on the campus of the boarding
school where our fathers taught. The summer of '76 stuck

to our tanned skin in the boredom of long,
humid days in PA. The radio reported record heat
waves that year. On Saturdays we were trapped
inside until the house was *redd up*, a command
in her Pittsburghese to clean up. She knelt

down by our side on hardwood floors, a bucket
of Murphy oil soap at her hip.
Row upon row of washed out
photographs of our ancestors
in the hills of San Martino peered
down from the mantel. Yet

this was the hour when other faculty kids began
to scent the chlorine in the campus pool.
Other than swimming,
the small coal mining town down the mountain
across the Kiskiminetas river offered little distraction.

Led by her quick hands around the house, we scrubbed
the bathroom tub with Clorox, vacuumed
rugs, wiped clean the bottom
of kitchen drawers. By late August
the noon heat clutched the wilting
wallpaper. I'd grumble,
is Nana coming to stay for the week? In silence

she would just work alongside me mopping
the steep stairs, smiling consent. In the bedrooms
my older sisters lip synched
Diana Ross' *Ain't No Mountain High Enough*
on the hi-fi, squabbled over whether Patty Hearst
was faking Stockholm Syndrome. Downstairs
my brother wisecracked
about the neighbor's slutty daughter. All this banter

in the house was like music to her. Only
years later did we find out
that she did not know how to swim.
At the time what we could not know
was how her Saturday cleaning ritual held
us in place next to her, wavering

in the heat where no one could sink
to the bottom of the deep end of the pool.

Caregiver

He has walled me in so I cannot escape;
he has weighed me down with chains.
Lamentations 3:7

Hours waiting for tests at the hospital
with my sister have stopped,
no more treatment to endure up
the nose, down the throat
with full-blown AIDS peaking
like the narcissus I forced
last January. Smoothing out the bedspread,
she tries her best to switch the mood
something will come along.
I miss the days of protest at ACT-UP

demonstrations in Harvard Square. Instead
I'm left flat on my back, my bones no longer padded.
Much of the time I just

listen to sounds of distant
street noise, her coming
and going. Throughout

the day we speak through the shorthand
of gestures, a nod, a wave, a wink, much
as we did as teenagers when we hid

secrets from our parents. I pretend
to be brave after all, attempt
to play the role of staying
alive. Yet counting off all I've lost,
I cannot sleep off
this fear. I try to hide

it from her, use my eyes,
my smile, but my expressions misfire.
Underneath our evening chitchat, the pulsing
thing that is true: I will not
outlast it this time. Only now
am I ready to let go of her hand.

Lot's Confession
Genesis 19:1-29

In the night air the city square
was falling fire, my eyes stitched
in burning, the last chance
to break out. I had to put
an end to it, my daughters offered
to strangers at the gate
the day before, the girls squinted
at me twisting their braided
hair. Up the mountain, my wife crossed
her hands, tight fisted
against her stomach, wrapping
her sadness in the folds
of her blue dress when she turned back
to head down to the bones
of our baby boy in the burial ground.
Longing for the life she left behind
came clawing back to her,
stronger than any punishing
commandment. She stored up
the loss of our child
year after year, tending
to the fevered past.
After his death I tucked myself away
in the shadows of the market
selling fresh figs, nursed
a deaf spot that could not
hear what was unsaid
by her hot kitchen stove.

Over the mountains
my daughters lagged behind
from the beginning, rocks
rough on their feet,
so I clutched their arms
on the steep cliffs. *Holding on*
would cost another life,
I yanked them forward, vanishing
over the hilltop
away from the smoke
drowning Gomorrah,
relieved how much bigger
the stars became in the black sky.

Section 3

Gin Rummy

In the summer of Carter's oil crisis,
I'm sprawled on my stomach
on the back porch, *The Hobbit* cracked
open. Her easel hovers over me, oil paints mingle
with honeysuckle that flirts up
on the breeze. Now that dishes are washed,
my mother lights up a Marlboro, settling
in the orange lawn chair, her crossed leg
jiggles, her freckled arm stretching for the worn
deck of cards on the banister. *Let's play gin rummy,*
shuffling with her strong knuckles before dealing. I scan
the ten cards held tight to my chest.
There's no three of a kind in my hands, no cards of the same suit
in sequence. *Learn to have more of a poker face,* whispering
to me through her exhale of smoke
that scribbles in the air. On my turn to pick up,
no cards of the same rank.
I discard the five of clubs. No straight
flush after drawing again. *Let's start
over,* I blurt out. But mother just
sweet-talks me, *you'll never be dealt
a perfect hand, play the cards you're dealt.*

Solitaire

I finish what is left
in the whiskey bottle.
Sit down to solitaire
at the kitchen table
set for one, always
with a single deck,
just how my mother taught
me when I was ten.
I like how the game
is played
by oneself, the way
the cards are laid out
from the start,
some in rows,
some in columns,
mixing reds and blacks.
Minor blemishes
on the queen of hearts,
a light thumbmark
on the five of spades,
a trace of tiny bits
of food on the jack
of diamonds.
I wait for the right
suit, each card
flipping over,
no matches
falling into place.
I've come
to accept what
is put before me,
pitted against myself.

The blue hour

arrives. The late light turning
on me draws the day closer, the east
meadow beyond the grove of birches, some animal
stirring at the edge of sight. Peering out,
I let loose like the wind
riffling through the trembling ferns after two days
of rain. In places only whispering birds fly to, everything
collapses into green shadows, my eyes
adjusting to the faceless dark.
                              I remember a time being afraid
of it, even when I was most hidden. Now it feels safe,
the way the perfected dark lets it all pass
without comment, marking each thing.
                                    What I wanted
earlier out of this day stalled under the summer sun,
my stubborn seeing only one thing at a time. Everything
in the growing blackness declares itself, unlocking the night.
Something looks back from the flickering
leaves, knows me for who I am.

Christmas Eve, 2001
Luke 2:7-9

After the swollen party I sit up alone, wide-awake
sipping eggnog spiked with Barbados rum. Darkness

keeps coming on outside. Blue lights on the silent
tree vibrate in the corner of the room,

carols play on FM radio at midnight interrupted
by news reports on strikes up in the Afghan mountain

range. I mouth *shepherds watch their flock
by night* under my breath. Out

on the snowy banks herders have not
been warned of King Herod's decree.

How many stars did they see in the blind
sky that night, everything ripe in the moonlight

before the raids? They heard the hoarse cough
of gunfire punctuated in the hills, their eyes drawn

to the red planet flaring above a mother and child, tucked deep
in a cave. The shepherds on the northern

slopes, too isolated to get word of the bloodshed down
in the villages, are nestled with their flock

on the border, stay up to trail the first light
spearing up the broken mountain

below a morning star, a rush
of tenderness for all they didn't know.

The Pond

The pond was so solid
that winter, the thick
ice sheet saved
us from falling through at that age.

On Christmas day at the cabin,
childhood memories turn up
unannounced. Funny what
time keeps for itself. On stiff

January days, our bundled
bodies prowled
the dawn rushing
to the pond to sweep
the ice smooth. My sister and I traced
each other's figure eights forward
and backward until our fingers turned
blue. I wouldn't expect to step back
into the cold perfection

of those early mornings. Certain adult
quarrels still flit around
my sister and me where we limped
away, stunned each other with words sharp
enough to crack through the unbroken
surface. Those sentences sound different

heard across the years, mistakes we can't make up
for. On this holiday sadness wafts

around me as I comb through an old album
for a Polaroid picture of her sometime
around 1973, her long chestnut hair twirled
behind her ears crisscrossing the ice toward
me. Digging up this snapshot peels away

how I forfeited many years that were plunged
under the weight of our lives apart.

K5, (P10, K10) repeat to last 5sts, K5
knitting pattern for a baby blanket

Your voice unspools inside me knitting
on the porch while bats crisscross
the yard. The blow-up

that morning at Dad's funeral is as burnished
as a scar on that old elm tree we used to play kick
the can under. I'm halfway through a blanket
for a friend's baby, using lopi wool
skeins hunted down in Iceland

last winter. I thought we had reached
a truce in that old family quarrel. Yet
my fingers will not
allow me to rest, the wooden
needles ticking knit 10, purl 10
into a basket
weave design. Just

now I have lost count
of the rows and notice a dropped

stitch, a hole at the top. I won't
deny how hurt
blossoms over the years, but you have developed
a kind of affection for your airtight
anger. Tonight, I'll spend

time unpicking, unraveling yarn
row by row to get back to where the pattern
went wrong, pulling apart
the tangled knots.

Tableau

I do remember the last conversation
with my father in the hospital room, though
I cannot put it down word for word.

I have no control
over my memory of him now. Just

this morning it came back to me, for no good reason,

his Dunlop tennis racquet
leaning up against the striped
wallpaper in the foyer, the rosewood pipe
that rested on the glass ashtray next
to the ivory chest set, his special books shelved
on the Winthrop desk. Still

remember his face at fifty
when I was only nine, the details are less sharp
so I shuffle through old
photographs to fill them in.

His heavy voice was a constant in my head
for more than forty years. Today
I know his absence in the same way,
or when I hear his words drift
out of my mouth.

December Night

The trees know first. An ice storm is moving in.
I'm still holding back trouble I've carried
around in my mind for two days. Yet
some worries are always there. Must admit
it has felt like an empty year. At midnight
I come to bed in pitch black, but nothing
brings relief in the clinging cold.
All night I live with cracking branches, the wind
refusing to die down, and still awake
at four a.m. with my brain beating
under this blurred sky. The slim birches, stripped
of color, flex down and over in the freezing
darkness. Then the sky clears, the white
trunks straighten by dawn, as in any storm.

First Day Of Winter

Behind the cabin a red moon stares through the birches, calmed
by the dark. Night covered in wide stillness, these trees slurring
no loud speech. Earlier in the day gunshots in the distance rung
through empty trees. I settle back inside, waiting for dawn
on this first day of winter. I have fought long in these woods,
coaxing the quiet inside me to come nearer. In a world buried
under the cold surface, nothing is forced out easily. Darkness
in this corner hides me, a space to be safe in. Outside
the wind has picked up rising and falling back
in the sky as if to let something out. Behind the frozen pane
the day glistens on the windowsill, tracks of deer in the creased
snow. How close they came while I was sleeping.

While You Were Away
a letter to Jon

Last night I dreamt I spoke to you
in fluent Italian, foreign
words that fell over us like confetti
struggling for a language to keep
us together. I had lost

all recall of English grammar, groping for another lexicon
to explain myself to you. You squinched

your face in confusion. Instead
conversed in German--*schlecht, zeit*-- sounds striking
at me thick and sharp as hail. You and I were trapped
in an immense distance between vocabularies, sentences back
and forth that dragged us down. I jotted
down German verbs to look up. You corrected

my conjugations and tenses. Why is the verb
to be irregular in almost
every language? What did you intend

to confess that could not be put
in our native tongue? Reactions had become
a Scrabble board of unknown words scattered
like tiles on the upstairs game
table. And then I woke.

You returned late last night after nursing
your father in California. Nearing three decades, nestled
in our bed, my body filled with your breath
in a weightless silence, saying more than anything we hoped
to say, my mouth pressed word
for word on you.

Losing Ernie

Just this week I brought myself to shake off
your fur trapped on the green blanket
you lounged on. Nighttime treats
still rest on the edge of my bedside
table. I'm writing this now so not

to lose you to time. Or am I writing
to bury you after holding on to your ashes
these last four months? Your leaving was such

a surprise. To keep grief at bay, I started to knit
again, trying hard to move forward

with the quiet click
of the wooden needles, the warmth of the yarn
on my lap. After picking out a dropped
stitch, I pull out three rows, my fingers rubbing the skein
as if it were your fur coat up against
my thigh on the sofa. Nothing takes it away.

You framed the day. Your morning egg heated up
on the stove, taking you out
to the Boston Public Garden
when I came home from work, the stroll
around Marlborough Street
at night, and your last treat
of the day that I always gave to you on the bed
before sleep.

Losing you has undone
me, passing by the last photograph I took
of you, your pug head tilted
to the left from late
stages of the brain tumor, catching a hint
of your scent still on a chair pillow.
I know the dead do not return,

yet they also never fully leave. Did I hold on tight

enough to you that final month? Yesterday I came upon
the bald man with his dachshund out
on the Boston Common who was unsure whether to ask
about you not walking along
side me. We only know the names
of each other's dogs, not of each other.

My partner is feeding the neighborhood
dogs your favorite peanut butter biscuits.
Before the early morning visit
to the vet on December 22nd, your breathing was labored
for three hours. I confess I prayed
secretly, *let Ernie die, let it not*
get to the point where we must put him to sleep.

Now there is no there
where I can find you in a patch
of sun on the daybed, yet
you are still un–losable.

A Turn In The Year

Late September. Raking the flower beds that have gone
to seed, I take in the lowing of the herd moving down
the hillside, their meadow hayed late this season after the long
rains. The rutted dirt road up to their sagging barn pulls me away
from turning over the soil. The evening cold is coming,

their purposeful eyes pressed up against the fence stop
to stare in my direction, nodding as I walk
away from summer. I turn to autumn, a wind carrying pain
covered over after years of separation from a sister like smoke
from a battle, now lined up in my throat

leaking out, and at last these cows hear me voice them aloud.
My body leans into their calm animal
inhale and exhale, blowing out fears that fall
away with the cattle's breath. Back in the garden, I push
the shovel down hard, in deep and heave the earth open.

November Dark

The morning begins dressed in layers in the November dark.
The Christmas cactus peaks on my desk. With trees scrubbed

clean moving into winter, I draw the cabin around
me like a shawl shrouding disappointment in the last
year, the erosion of a long friendship, stumps left from worn out
resentments. I have not seen a blue sky
in four days, and two more days until J. returns

from France. So many times, this year everything came undone.
Plans to visit an estranged sister were made, came apart
by Ernie's passing in its place, new delights popped up
traveling to Ghent and Bruges last spring. The forecast
calls for three inches of snow by nightfall.
Fretting hour by hour, I strip

the sheets, stoke the fire, put out suet
for the birds, chores in a bid
to master the personal uncertainty
that plagues me. By late afternoon with the scent
of wood smoke in the air, nothing is left
to tidy, shuffling housework to quell

old losses. Time to pull my mind up
to the surface leaning over a notebook,
and let dusk settle on my desk
as I write myself back together again.

Winter Journal

For a long time now,
I have not spoken. Even
in April, wind cuts
my face in this vague light.
Still little warmth
in the sun. Snow has shriveled
out on the meadow. In another week,

a quick melt. Meanwhile
my heart thumps in these tossing
trees set loose to the rhythm
of the clouds that move west
over the mountains carrying
cold rain. Geese fly close over the surface
of the pond. Slumped in this fallow
field, what an effort
to move through the silence. Only by chance,

my fingers stub on some roots
under an old stone wall, bulbs

start to crawl up my throat, gurgling
laughter for no reason.

Monologue
Sunday morning, late December

Just look out at daybreak into the blending
landscape under a pink sky. Talk to a dead
father who drifts in through the silence.
There on the mantel, settle on the Christmas cactus
in full bloom---alive, alive after another bitter cold
night. Rest at the bare table, a page of warm light
pouring yellow over the teacup. Afterwards
make your way outside where the slender poles
of white birches tip forward, spilling their soft-packed
white flakes in winter's patchy sunlight. Take in
what's going on all around you, breaking
yourself open in the hush out in the deserted
field that is like the snow in the air.

Reading My Father

By December with your death not yet a habit,
a box of books arrives that you asked
my sister to pack up for me. I pull out

Raccontini Italiani on top, open
to the dedication page, notes scrawled in Italian
in your curly cursive, the ink of a felt tip pen faded.

I placed distance between us that last year, not prepared
to let what was happening to you reach me, controlling
the itinerary of my visits to Pittsburgh.

In the Reagan years I lived closed off
to you, covered up with my silence, no
choice to be free in the white space of coming out.

Unpacking this box, my hands hold
your favorite books again that are now the last
of you, read lines until I hear your voice as it was in life, leaf

through the margins of dog-eared pages, underlined
passages where you penciled in my name,
and I recover you one notation at a time.

Walter, Pierre, Tim, Howard

We had a good rain all night, their names crashing down
from the past. Thirty years later from up

here in this bedroom window, I see across the wide
lawn where everything in these gardens goes on
at such a fast pace...the lilacs,
peonies, roses. The new delight, purple phlox
blooming late in the cool mountain
air. For some time now I've not spoken

their names, young men who hungered
for the world they were losing, and what
in their leaving, they took. They died
without funerals. We gave away
their clothes to Goodwill, all of them we outlived.
At the time did not know how much we had yet
to lose in the AIDS epidemic.

On this ordinary summer day, you and I surround
ourselves with a cabin in the woods, a pug
called Ernie, all tokens of permanency. What

forced me to remember their names last night?
I suppose because it would take a blunt
act of excision to forget. These decomposing

flower beds remind me that nothing in this world
keeps, nothing but my memory intact.

Last Will And Testament

for a niece

I imagine how puzzled
my niece will be as she tries to make
sense why I collected these tchotchkes,
held on to over time. Painted
eggs from Estonia's Russian
Church in bowls on end
tables, Scandinavian
miniature houses crowded
on mantles. I have no doubt
this volcanic rock or that chachka carried
back from Iceland will be stuffed
in black plastic bags put out
on garbage day, all these small
fragments fastening me to a certain
time. Will she be curious to trace
my steps in Rome or Helsinki, filling in
what she did not know about me? Still
I fret over what will come of this twisted
driftwood balanced on a slim
windowsill offered as an engagement
ring by Jon after hiking all afternoon
on the cliffs above Goat Rock
Beach. She'll stuff old
Dutch tiles found in Ghent, antique
plates once hung
above doorways in jam-packed
cardboard boxes. Will she dismiss
my happiness in the company of these silent
things when she drops
off boxes and bags at Goodwill or Salvation
Army? I know I clung

to all these remnants cluttered
around the house, this great
need somehow to keep
that time of my life, that certain
feeling. Will she know why?
Because we cannot stay.

Cattle

Coal eyes stared back
at me in the dark, their massive heads tilted
to one side, how I imagine the dead
must see us. The harvest moon

at midnight pulled me out
of bed. I stood barefoot on the dirt
road, the meadow wet with dew
where they had come out
of the barn, their brown coats glazed
in moonlight. In the cool
air they pressed together like capuchin
monks at compline. No gestures
or words to exaggerate the black
silence, even the full moon dimmed
the burning stars. These cattle

had no buzz in their head,
no urge to wish it were not so,
no shame to fill their long evenings.

I was comforted to know these giant
maples that line this farm will be here long
after I am gone. Over the fence face to face
with these animals, their eyes followed
me as I walked out
of the light, making out in the dark

just another being moving in the world,
appearing then as I truly am
under the night sky.

The Chipped Vase
five months into lockdown

I take out the withered stalks, making room
for the crumpled blossoms that hold on,
replace the water stinking in the chipped
vase, everyday housework that hinges on the smallest
chore accomplished. Most days I keep
sane by some routine like putting clean sheets on a bed,
weeding a garden border, drawn to work
that carries the promise of daily progress, hovering
around something that just might
reveal itself. By mid-day after tea, I settle on what
is left of the afternoon light on the stone
wall, animal presences frisking out of the undergrowth
at the edge of the woods, this new life made up
of little joys chained like daises, one by one.

Monhegan Island, August

On a lumpy bed we talk in near dark
by an open window and let
the darkness collect, making
the room more private. You cup
the back of my neck, my hairline turning
gray in the last year. I sweep the bangs
from your forehead. A plain tenderness
tumbles between us. And we fall asleep.
After waking, we gripe about how long
this stretch of weather has gone on.
We wait all morning for the sun.
Rain has lasted two weeks, creeping
behind us wherever we go.

Middlefield, 7.14.12

Late at night as we sleep into one another
on this sagging bed, the mattress sloping
us to your side, I think

of our years together, the room
still as though it were holding its breath
for the next sentence soft-spoken.

I hear in the night what the house has to say,
listen to our conversations in disrepair. Only tonight
after brushing the Scrabble letters into the cardboard box
at the end of the game have I shuffled
each strained-for word of our exchanges in the kitchen.

Despite the hour, I want to rouse you.
Whisper to you about the way the dark
holds on, how the rhythmic croaking vibrates out
in the meadow. A cool draft separates the curtains lifting up
enough for me to show you a heavy moon
taped up in the sky.

The crisp scent of spearmint seeps in
from the window cracked open, the sweep

of the raw wind sifting the leaves. By your side I lie there finding
a voice, call out in a language
more actual than speech.

For once, I admit words fail me, shrivel away in my mouth.

Let me draw you out of bed into the mountain
air, our eyes making out the steady pulse
of a firefly under this starless night
on the other side of words.

Lines On Autumn Day

My level gaze out the window keeps an eye
on chickadees perched together, feather
to feather, at the feeders hung in early October.
I recognize in their pecking at the suet,
in their darting back and forth to nests
in the pines, my own grasping and letting go.
By midday the temperature is falling, light
crosses from east to west earlier in the afternoon
over the empty trees. First, I must thin out
my own regrets, to tie the frayed rope ends of holding on
and releasing. Maple trees that line the yard drop
the last of their blood dipped leaves. Today I swear
to let everything settle where it will,
wherever that is.

August Hymn

Let everything remain
as it is, the unexpected quiet
like the August heat out
in the meadow, the sun rubbing
the old maples. Look at the black-eyed
Susans studded along the dirt road
dropping open as they lose their tight
grip. Do not hurry. Nothing
about this day asks
to be changed, things being just
as they are. Come,
let us breathe in unison
with the cattle in their long
stare across the creek
on this fine Sunday morning slipping away,
this day we cannot hold on to,
taking whatever comes like the drifting
hawk that rises in the sky. Kneel down
in the tall grass in simple perfection
with the humming
of the almond-eyed grasshoppers
before the farmer's last baling.
Blessings waft
through the summer air. Little by little,
leave the other voices behind. Stop
right here, right now
to listen to the wood thrush repeat
its four fluty notes, calling up
I'm here, I'm here.

Acknowledgements

Special gratitude to Dr. Rockwell Gray, my first poetry mentor, and to poet David Semanki, my initial reader and supporter of my writing.

(Journals in which poems in this collection were originally published, many of which have undergone revision.)

The Rift: The Deronda Review
On The Front Porch: The Chaffin Journal (Eastern Kentucky U.)
Monehegan Island, August: Willard and Maple
After The Phone Call: Timber Creek Review
Us: Sierra Nevada College Review
There is nothing to do now but wait (Originally published as Notebook, 1978): Common Ground Review
Family Dinner, 1972: The Chaffin Journal (Eastern Kentucky U.)
First Bike: The Comstock Review
Man To Man: Gertrude Journal
The Sick Bed: Common Ground Review
Solitaire, Mirror, and Mission Hill, AIDS Hospice: The MacGuffin
Mission Hill, AIDS Hospice: nominated for Best Poets by The
     MacGuffin
Red Line: Clark Street Review
Winter Journal: Abbey
The blue hour: Cider Press Review
Copenhagen: Tiger's Eye
Middlefield, 7.14.12: Common Ground Review
Housekeeping: The Old Red Kimono
That First Summer: Writer's Bloc
Sunday Phone Call: Peregrine Journal
Ahab's Crew: Rockford Writer's Guild
Monologue: Caveat Lector
That First Summer: The Griffin
Lot's Confession: Peregrine Journal
from a summer journal: The Old Red Kimono

About The Author

Anthony Botti grew up in western PA and holds a Master of Divinity from Harvard Divinity School. His poetry has appeared in The Comstock Review, The MacGuffin, Cider Press Review, Flint Hills Review, and Mudfish. Over the last 25 years he has worked in behavioral health administration serving students, staff, and faculty at Harvard University Health Services. He divides his time between Boston and the Berkshires with his partner and their pug, Puck.